OCTO, PI

AND THE MISSING EGG

A ZAR&R Mystery

A ZAR&R Mystery

OCTO, PI

AND THE MISSING EGG

Sarah McDavis

Paperback: 979-8-9905158-0-2

eBook: 979-8-9905158-1-9

Book Cover and illustrations by Sarah McDavis

Published by Wonder Creek Media, Pittsburgh, PA

Visit us at www.wondercreekmedia.com

1st edition 2024

For my family,
my best cheerleaders

Pssst!! We call this place the Zar and r. The full name is a tongue twister!

Welcome to the
ZAR&R
Zoological and Aquatic Rehabilitation and Research Center
Comic foot-drawn by Lightning
Hiya! Lightning here!
I have so much to tell you about the ZAR&R!
First, there are all kinds of residents here. Some of us live here full time. Like Octo and me and Tank.
This is Tank. He's Octo's assistant and usually blending in somewhere.
Others leave after they get what they need.
Some need rest. Others need medicine and care.
Next, there are a lot of different habitats here.

Here's a map of the ZAR&R:
These paths separate the ecosystems.
Pond
Treetop Terrace
Octo's Home Office
I don't use the paths, faster to fly, you know?
Last, I need to tell you about Octo, PI. She's not a sucker, but her arms are full of them.
Octopus suckers
Octo likes facts that stick!
#1 case solver at the ZAR&R
Octo, PI
Species
Veined Octopus
Pronouns
she/her
Time to go get the buzz around the ZAR&R! If something happens, Octo will need the facts!

1

KNOCK KNOCK HONK!

I almost inked.

"What in the name of seashell pajamas?"

I climbed out of my seawater tank. My morning swim would have to wait. I reached for my spectacles, careful not to stick a sucker on the glass. Sucker rings are very difficult to clean, let me tell you.

*KNOCK KNOCK **HONK!***

I knew that honk. What had made her so impatient?

"Just a moment!" I quickly dried up the puddle I had made. Eight arms means a big puddle and puddles are not professional.

*KNOCK KNOCK **HONK!***

"Come in!" I called before she broke down the door.

Mama Goo burst in as I knew she would. She usually stood proudly at a height of more than eight clownfish. But today her long neck drooped and her black beak quivered. Her signature wicker basket was covered in stray feathers.

"How can I help you, Mama Goo?" I asked. I knew to never call her Mother Rhymes-With-Moose. That name really ruffled her feathers, and an angry goose is NOT someone you want to be around. Especially near a tank of water. It is so hard to get that wet feather smell out.

I grabbed my notepad and seven gel pens, one for each arm. I liked to color code my notes.

I offered Mama Goo my clamshell chair.

"Oh, I couldn't possibly sit at a time like this. One of my eggs has been stolen!"

I was about to ask why she assumed her egg was stolen, but she kept honking. Mama Goo had been known to **accuse** first and ask questions later.

"It's that stranger next door. Her moving in is the only new thing by the pond. I am sure she has taken it!"

> Side Note:
> When someone accuses someone else, they are saying the other person did something wrong. But they might not have all the facts.

"Did you see her take the egg?" I asked. It's always good to start with the facts.

"No," Mama Goo honked, "but how

else would it have gone missing?"

I needed a timeline of events. I asked, "When did you notice the egg was gone?"

"At sunrise. I was counting my eggs before going to breakfast, as I always do. But today, one was missing. In all my egg-laying years, I have never had a missing egg before! I know that stranger must have taken it!"

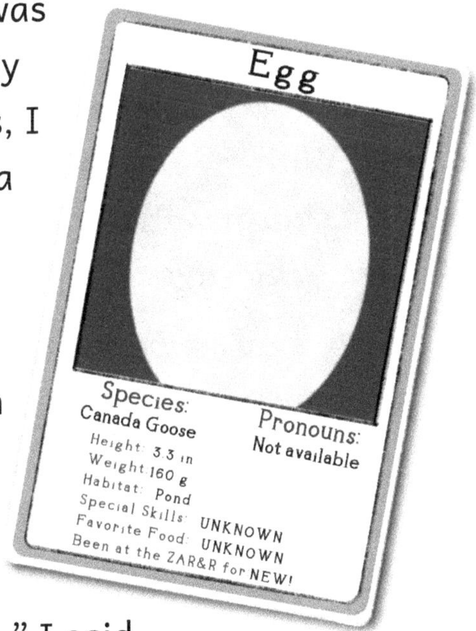

"We don't know that, Mama Goo," I said,

trying to calm her down. "What kind of animal moved in?" My first guess was a raccoon or maybe a fox that hadn't yet learned the rules around here. What Mama Goo said next surprised me more than finding a crab in a cantaloupe.

"Well..." Mama Goo looked puzzled. "I saw her for only a moment. She was gone in a flash. With my egg, no doubt! I was sure I heard a slap of water, like those beavers last year, remember?"

Oh, I remember, I thought. That wasn't the question Mama Goo wanted answered, though.

"She's some kind of furry... Well, I just can't put my feather on it," she continued. "All I know is she stole my egg!"

And she shut her beak.

Mama Goo was speechless.

Well, almost speechless.

"Octo, you must help me get it back," she said. She pulled two clam crumpets out of her wicker basket and set them on my desk. "And before it gets cold and dark!"

"Okay, Mama Goo, Octo, PI, will take the case," I announced. I would have taken the case regardless. Missing eggs need to be found, after all. But the clam crumpets sealed the deal. She knew they were my favorite.

I showed Mama Goo to the door.

"I'll be searching around my nest," she said over her shoulder. "I need to keep watch over my other eggs. I couldn't stand it if another was stolen."

Of course she had to have the last word.

2

"Sounds mysterious there, boss."

For the second time in less than an hour, I almost inked.

I spun around to what looked like an empty room. I wasn't scared. Not me. Just a little concerned, was all. Mysteries, I liked. Surprises in my home office, not so much.

"It's just me, boss," said my clamshell chair.

Last I checked, clamshell chairs didn't talk. Being a master puzzle solver, I knew who was actually doing the talking.

"Tank, we discussed this," I said. "No camouflage in here. What if Mama Goo had sat on you? What if I had?"

The idea of a chameleon dotted and sore from sucker spots was not appealing. Not to mention, if I had sat on him, I surely would have inked.

Two eyes appeared on my clamshell chair.

"Sorry, boss," Tank said, "I've been practicing."

His tightly curled tail slowly started changing color from the tip. It spiraled from pink and cream to blue. Then a wave of neon washed across his body as if someone had thrown paint on him. I had to admit his skills in disguise were improving. The shades of the shell were difficult to match so perfectly. I should know—I've tried.

"Perhaps we can save those skills for the field and not my office," I said. Tank smiled. He nodded as he kept one eye on me and one on the window. It had taken me a while to adjust to Tank's eyes looking in different directions. In our line of work, it comes in very handy.

Tank and I had worked a number of cases together. He was one of the most informed animals at the ZAR&R. Like Mama Goo and me, he was here for a lifetime of R&R. The other animals tended to forget he was around when they were talking, on account of him blending in so well. You might say he became like part of the furniture.

"What's the word in the trees, Tank?" I asked. "Any whispers about a goose egg on the loose?"

"This is the first I've heard about it," Tank answered. His eye that pointed in my direction darted all over, searching behind me. He always checked each possibility. One thing was certain, the egg was not in my home office. "With how loud Mama Goo was honking on about it, the whole place is bound to have heard by now."

Mama Goo surely wasn't one to keep her opinions about anything to herself.

But I didn't work in opinions. I worked in facts. And the only two facts I knew were:

1) a goose egg was missing
2) we had a new arrival

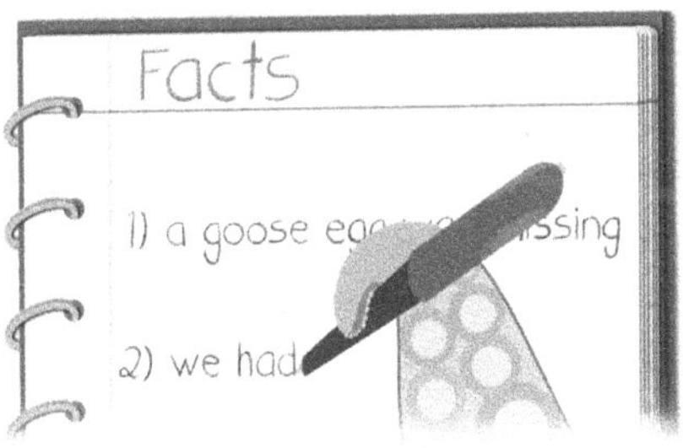

I didn't yet know if they were connected. I needed more facts. I flipped to a blank page in my notepad.

"What have you heard about this new neighbor Mama Goo talked about?" I asked. Tank swiveled both his eyes in my direction. I had his full attention now. This was a very interesting possible **suspect**.

Side Note:
A suspect is someone who may have broken a rule in a case. Our new mystery neighbor had been accused, but we need more facts.

"Yesterday, I overheard the ducks mention a new arrival," Tank said. "But I don't think they were quacking about the same one Mama Goo says stole her egg."

"Why do you say that?"

"The ducks were definitely not discussing a beaver."

"Mama Goo didn't say it was a ..."

"SHHHH!" Both of Tank's eyes whirled toward the open window.

"Someone is c..."

He didn't finish his sentence because someone wasn't coming.

Someone was here.

3

Unlike Tank, Lightning always loved to make an entrance. Her wings beat so fast, she hummed louder than a swarm of bees. For someone so tiny, she effortlessly filled the space. My junior investigator flitted around my office faster than a seal fleeing an orca. Tank started blending into the background again. I tried to toss in a "Good Morning," but Lightning came in fast with

her report.

"Hiya, Octo! Hiya, Tank! It's a buzz out there today! There's a new resident the others can't make heads or tails of, you know. Well, that's part of it, I think. The head doesn't seem to match the tail and everyone is talking about it. Even over across the grassland plain. And they aren't ever interested in anything except eating. Every. Single. Blade. Of. Grass. You know. It's exhausting trying to talk to them. Anywho, I went over to the lake, as part of the welcoming crew, you know. The little critter was hiding under water. I'm pretty sure it's not a fish. But I'm not a hundred percent, no diving for me, you know. Can't fly if I get these beauties too wet."

I hung up Lightning's favorite sugar water tube on a hook by the window. She paused for a sip. I pulled my arm back in quickly because I never knew where she was going to fly next. Once, Lightning got too close to one of my suckers as she whizzed around the room. Turns out, a slime covered hummingbird can't fly either.

"Thanks for this info, Lightning. You sure have been busy."

"Anytime, Octo! I can be anywhere

and back with the **scoop** in a flash, you know.”

Side Note:
The scoop is the story. In this case, it's the mystery. Thankfully, Lightning always tried to stick to the facts. That helped me out heaps.

Unfortunately, none of Lightning’s information was going to help find Mama Goo’s missing egg. And that was what this case was about. Unless the egg and new arrival were connected somehow. I needed to find out.

“In all that talking around the Ol’ ZAR&R, any buzz about a missing goose egg?” I asked.

“Oh my! Well, Mama Goo’s honking on and on about how the new resident stole one of hers. The others around the pond aren't so quick to place the blame, but they are keeping a tighter watch on their nests. I noticed the herons standing around more than usual. I heard lots of what ifs and maybes, whispers on the wind, really, but nothing concrete. I'm looking for the facts, you know. Like you taught me, Octo."

She stopped for another sip.

"I can always count on you for the fast facts, Lightning."

"I thought I heard something from the red panda brothers as I flew by." Lightning took one more sip. "They were talking about an egg, I think. But I couldn't catch much of the conversation."

It would have surprised me if the brothers had taken the egg. They'd come to the ZAR&R around the same time I had. They knew the rules. At least, I thought they did. I hoped this wasn't one of their tricks.

I opened a new case file and transferred my notes. A different color for each category.

Crime: *Missing Egg*

Possible Suspects:

Mama Goo's new neighbor
(beaver/duck/fish hides underwater)

Red panda brothers???

Clues: *Mama Goo claims neighbor stole her egg,*

Red panda brothers might know something, no evidence at present

I pushed up my spectacles. I needed clues. Facts about what happened to the egg. Time to get into the field. I packed up the case file, my notebook, pens, and one of Mama Goo's clam crumpets. I put them safely under my hat. Luckily, with eight arms, packing is done in a flash. Almost as fast as Lightning.

"Okay team, let's go solve the mystery of the missing egg!"

It was time I saw this new resident for myself too. Either she was our main suspect or completely innocent. And it was my job to find out.

4

Lightning flew on ahead to the lake, but Tank and I don't move quite so fast. Underwater, I can really turn up my jets. On land, I need to be more creative.

I climbed in between two coconut shell halves.

"This isn't the time for bowling, boss," Tank joked as he climbed into his ride.

According to him, I looked like a ball ready to knock down some pins.

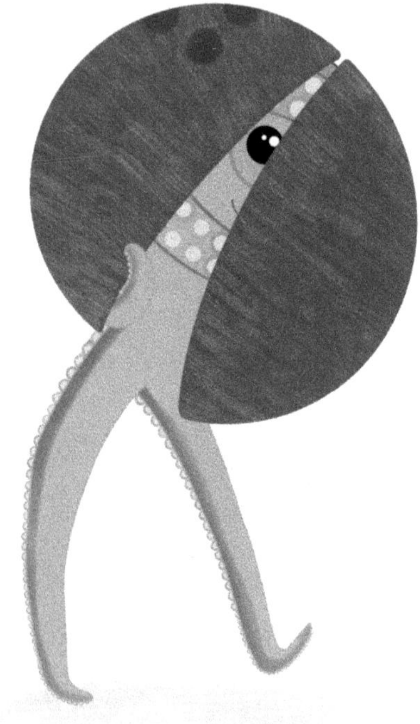

"I'm better at setting up pins, Tank," I said. Bowling shoes weren't made to fit these arms. Coconut shells, on the other **appendage**, were a perfect fit.

> Side Note:
> An appendage is an external body part. It could be a leg, a wing, or in my case, eight arms.

"When are you going to let me create something better for you to get around?" Tank asked. As good as he was at camouflage, Tank was an even better inventor. His homemade ride was a collection of parts and pieces he collected around the ZAR&R. It didn't look like much, but his ride was FAST. He was always trying to improve the situation with a new invention.

"I like my natural ride, thanks," I said. Every time I would think of climbing in a ride like Tank's, I worried about getting an arm stuck in a gear. Yikes, no thanks.

It was time to get moving.

I pulled the coconut shells almost closed. I left a crack for two arms to touch the ground like a pair of legs. Then I started to run. Once I reached my top speed, I drew in my arms and fully closed the shells around me. I was on a roll.

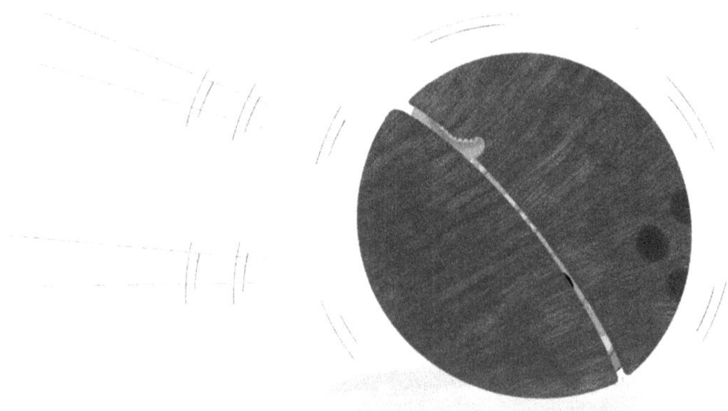

My home office was on one side of the ZAR&R as part of the aquarium. The lake where Mama Goo and the new resident lived was on the opposite side. The quickest route, if you weren't Lightning, of course, was the tunnel that ran under the habitats. It happened to be right next to the home of the red panda brothers.

I knew I needed to talk with them about what Lightning overheard. But Puck and Pan were as good at playing tricks as I was at solving mysteries. I wasn't keen on dealing with their tricks while looking for real clues. I would come back to talk with them after checking out the lake. That is, if I still needed more facts.

Tank rolled uneventfully into the tunnel, and I was right behind him.

Until...

"AHHH-EEE!" I screamed.

My shells went flying!

My arms flailed everywhere!

And I smacked into a patch of bamboo.

"Whoa! I give that..." yelled Puck.

"... a 9.45!" finished Pan.

The brothers looked down at me from their tree limb press box. I had rolled right up one of their ramp tricks.

"She was so close, but..."

"...needed more control on the landing to get that perfect score."

They were laughing so hard I thought they were going to fall out of their tree. I looked like an octopus shaped web.

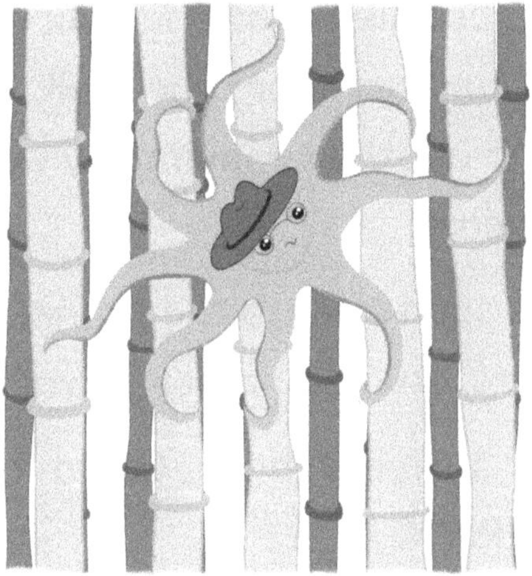

"You two jokers are interrupting official PI business!" Tank hollered as he turned a fiery red.

"Go on ahead and scout the scene, Tank," I said. "This sucker situation will take me a few minutes to unstick."

Bamboo patches and octopuses don't mix. The bamboo is so close together it's next to impossible to untangle all these arms. As I unstuck from one stalk, I would get stuck to another. Making my way out was slow going.

As Tank sped off into the tunnel, I heard the brothers' laughing quiet down.

"Official business, hmm. Could it be..." whispered Puck.

"...about an egg, perhaps?" finished Pan.

Now they had my full attention.

5

Red pandas love to eat bamboo. I have never known them to turn it down. It's a fact that they spend over half of their day looking for food. Here I found myself right in the middle of their favorite meal.

"Puck and Pan, could I get a paw?" I asked.

"I could use a snack, Pan," said Puck.

"I could, too, Puck," said Pan.

I watched the brothers turn and climb headfirst down the tree. Without any suckers! How they did that I wasn't sure, but I wouldn't be trying it that way.

The brothers sat down at the front of the bamboo patch. They curled their fluffy, striped tails around themselves. Then they tugged a stalk away from the others. This opened the patch up enough for me unstick my arms. I was thankful to reach the ground more quickly. Octopus arms are not very stretchy, let me tell you.

As they sat nibbling their snack, I picked up my coconut shells. But I couldn't leave yet. I had a feeling they had information I needed sooner rather than later.

"Have you fellas seen anything interesting lately? Perhaps over by the lake?" The brothers slowed their chewing. Now I seemed to have their attention.

Their eyes darted through the tunnel towards the pond and back to each other. They had definitely seen something. Were they going to give me the facts or try to trick me? I needed to find out.

"You mean besides a goose squawking her feathers off?" answered Pan.

"And a wingless duck with fur?" said Puck. His mouth was full of chewed bamboo.

I had enough of their tricks. I wouldn't be sidetracked by the sight of what looked like lumpy kelp in a blender. This was no time for me to be thinking about dessert. I needed to focus. It was past the middle of the day, and I didn't have enough facts yet to solve the case. I needed to find that egg. Sundown was coming.

"Not what I'm looking for, fellas, thanks anyway." Getting answers from them was harder than taking notes with a **sea pen**.

Side Note:
A sea pen is a living creature, not a thing to write with. They grow in the coral reef by my home office and they DO NOT like to be touched.

It was time for a trick of my own.

I rolled off in my coconut shells. Nothing followed me into the tunnel except the sound of the brothers' laughter. Once I was hidden in darkness, I propped my shells by the tunnel wall. I climbed up onto the ceiling and headed back toward the brothers.

Stone is not my favorite color to change into. I like brighter, bolder colors, myself. The grey and black specks helped

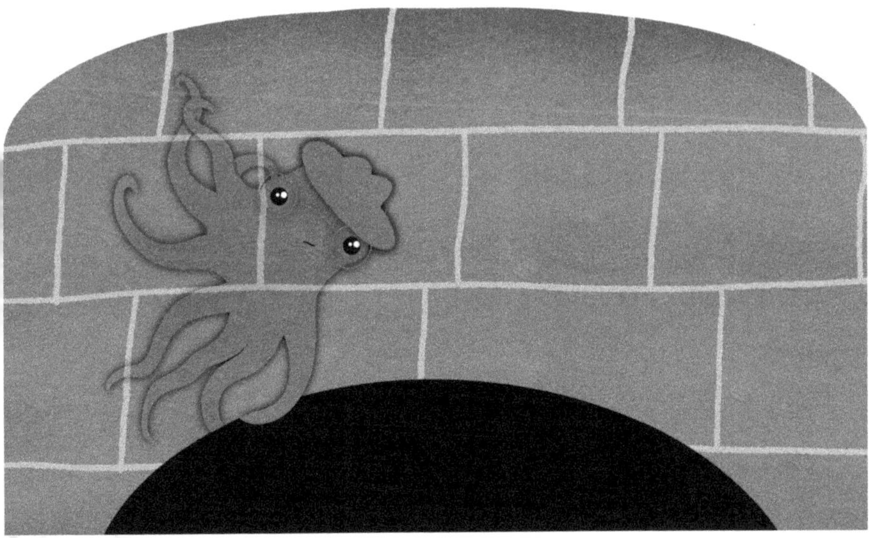

me blend in as I crawled back out of the tunnel. The brothers had stopped laughing. I could hear them loud and clear. Perfect, time to gets some facts, I thought.

"Maybe we should have told her..." Pan began.

"...about the egg?" Puck finished.

Pan shrugged.

"It was just an egg–" Puck started.

"WALKING BY ITSELF!" Pan shouted.

My suckers almost unstuck in shock.

Finally, a real clue!

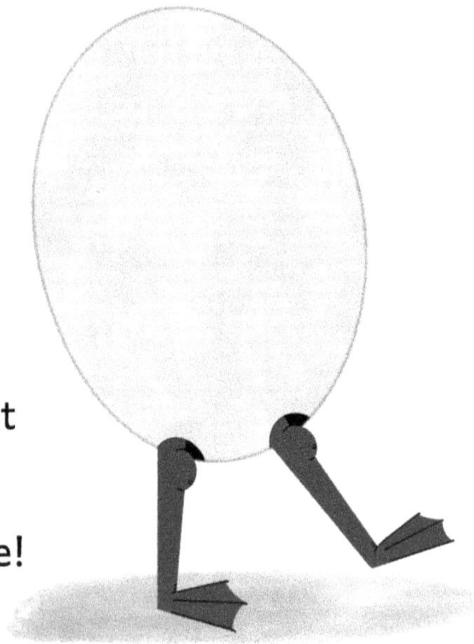

A clue that changed the whole case. Our possible suspects weren't suspects at all. Our mystery wasn't an egg-napping! It was a run-away. The egg could be anywhere, and it was all alone.

The sun was moving lower in the sky. I didn't have time to get stuck in another trickster trap. I needed their help.

"Puck? Pan?" I said. The brothers jumped as I changed to my normal color. "Did you put up any more tricks or traps up that way?"

"I'll show you," Pan said.

"NO!" Puck yelled.

"We'll show you," Puck said, leading the way into the tunnel.

Then I did something I never thought I

would do. I followed the red panda brothers into the tunnel. That walking egg needed to be found, and soon.

6

The lake was the biggest body of water at the ZAR&R. Mama Goo and other waterfowl lived there along with a whole slew of other residents. Reptiles, amphibians, mammals, and insects. Oh, the insects. It was just about time for all the insects to start waking up. The biggest group of them would be the mosquitos. Maybe tonight, octopus wouldn't be on their menu. It is so hard to scratch with just suckers, let me tell you.

Puck and Pan made it out first. It was a good thing they had helped because they had set up a trick inside the tunnel. Luckily, it didn't look like Tank had gotten caught in this one either.

"Thanks, fellas," I said.

"Anytime," said Pan.

"Hope you find that egg," said Puck.

The brothers climbed up a tree by the tunnel entrance to take the treetop route back home.

I needed to find Tank and Lightning. I heard the **commotion** before I

Side Note:
A commotion is a lot of noise and movement and in my experience doesn't have a lot of facts.

saw anything. Mama Goo was squawking even louder than this morning. Tank was trying, unfortunately ineffectively, to calm her down. Lightning was darting around what had to be the new neighbor.

I could see why the residents of the ZAR&R were talking about the new resident. She wasn't a beaver, but her tail looked like a beaver's. She wasn't a duck, but her beak looked like a duck's. She wasn't an otter, but her fur repelled the water droplets like otter fur. She wasn't like anything I had seen before. But she was mad. As mad as a moray eel being woken up from a nap.

It was time to investigate.

"You stole my egg! You egg stealer!" Mama Goo honked.

"I'm not an egg stealer!" the new neighbor yelled. "I'm a platypus! Why would I steal your eggs when I have my own?"

Another mystery solved. The new neighbor was a platypus.

I got Mama Goo's attention by waving two arms in her direction. "She did not steal your egg," I said.

"Of course she did. It's gone, isn't it?" Mama Goo started again.

"Your egg is missing, but she did not take it," I explained. "Witnesses saw your egg walk off by itself. She is not a suspect."

Mama Goo was speechless for the second time in one day. It might have been a record. I turned to the new neighbor.

"I'm sorry to meet you like this," I said. "I am Octo, PI."

"You can call me River," she said. Then she started to cry. Tank pulled over a lily pad to blow her beak on.

Before I could ask her why she was crying, Mama Goo found her voice again.

"Octo, we must find my egg. It's going to be dark soon. And it will get so cold. It could be anywhere. I'm so very worried about it."

She was right. Sundown was coming and fast. I needed clues to find the missing egg. Time to get cracking.

"Tank, talk to River and see if she saw a walking egg. Lightning, start a search for a self-propelled egg. I am going to check Mama Goo's nest for clues." Tank nodded and Lightning flew off.

Before I made it to the goose nest, Tank came running up behind me.

"Octo, we have a problem," he said. "Mama Goo isn't the only one missing someone. River had an egg go missing this afternoon."

He was right. This was a problem.

The case had just doubled. Two missing young ones and no new clues.

I waved Lightning in and told her the news.

"You got it, Octo. I'll keep my eyes open for two eggs somehow moving on their own. We'll find them soon, you know. You always solve the mysteries around here." She zoomed off to continue her search.

It was good to have Lightning's confidence in my abilities. I hoped she was right.

7

Sometimes the best way to solve a problem is to start at the beginning.

I knew the goose egg had walked off on its own. I started looking for tracks at Mama Goo's nest. I sent Tank and Lightning with River to look for more.

Luckily, none of the other eggs in the goose nest had sprouted legs. Mama Goo's webbed footprints were easy to spot. They circled her nest. One round on top of another. There were also three webbed print paths leading away from the nest. One set off toward my home office. Another led the way toward River's. The last one zigged and zagged. It made a few loops and headed into the tall grass.

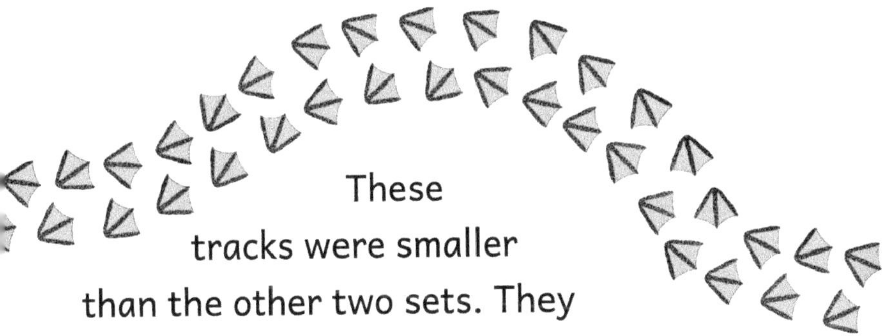

These tracks were smaller than the other two sets. They must have been made by the missing goose egg!

I followed the smaller tracks. They twisted and turned. Sometimes they went back and forth over themselves. The shell probably made it difficult to walk straight. But it should have been able to keep the gosling safe.

The tracks led me closer to the lake's edge. The mud was wetter there and any tracks the missing goose egg had made were long gone.

"Pssssst."

For the third time in a day, I almost inked.

"Pssst, over here."

I had been so focused on looking for tracks, I'd forgotten to look for witnesses to talk to. I followed the sound of the voice to the lake edge. The mud stuck inside my suckers. I tried to move quickly and quietly.

Unfortunately, each time I moved an arm, it sounded like a xylophone of pops.

"Keep it down, will ya? I don't want to wake up the frogs. I'm too majestic to be a meal."

Right at the water's edge, a lily pad washed ashore with a small passenger.

"I've seen what I think you are looking for," the dragonfly said.

The dragonfly's wings shimmered in the soon-to-be-setting sun. Two huge eyes covered most

of his head. With eyes like that, hopefully he would have some helpful clues. I pulled out my notebook and picked a blue pen to match the dragonfly. I nodded for him to continue.

"Earlier today, I saw an egg walk by," he said. "It almost walked into the water, but one little WHIRL-OOOP and it spun away from the edge."

So the goose egg was here! It was time to ask a few questions.

"Thanks for the tip," I said. "Did you follow the egg or see where it went?"

"I watched it walk toward the grass by the cattails over there. That was the last I saw of it."

"Did you see or hear anything else out of

the ordinary?" If the dragonfly saw the goose egg, perhaps he noticed the missing **puggle** too.

"There was goose honking all day that made it impossible to hear much of anything else," the dragonfly said. "And after that egg left, I tried to get a little midday nap in."

Side Note:
Yes, River said a baby platypus is called a puggle. It would be cuter if it wasn't missing.

"Thank you for your help." I put my notebook and pen away under my hat. I started through the sticky mud to the cattail grove. I streamlined my arms so I didn't end up tangled again.

I was about to start my search for tracks

again when Lightning came zooming past.

"Oh, Octo! I'm so glad I found you! We were tracing the small tracks from River's. Thank goodness it didn't rain today, or we would have been out of luck, you know? We found the eggs! Well, we found the eggshells, but we didn't see the gosling or the puggle anywhere."

8

Lightning led the way to the eggshells they'd found. She flitted in a zigzag pattern so I could keep up. That bird is fast!

When we arrived, Tank was standing guard over the broken shells. His eyes darted back and forth watching the crowd form. Word had

definitely gotten out now. The Creature Connect Broadcasting Network would be here any minute with their cameras.

"Stay away from the **scene**," Tank said. He guided the residents away from the shells and the water's edge. Lightning joined him so I could focus on the clues.

Side Note:
A scene is a location where something has happened or is happening. In this case, the scene is where two walking eggs hatched.

Why did the shells split open at this particular spot? I wondered. There were no big rocks or trees for them to hit. Then I remembered they had been following the tracks from River's. I had an idea forming. I needed to collect the facts to make sure I was right. I studied the ground closely.

Thankfully, the ground wasn't sticky or muddy, only damp. The tracks weren't hard to find. I followed the winding gosling tracks around in circles. But they weren't the only webbed footprints. Two sets of tracks tangled up in the damp ground.

The gosling tracks wobbled around in sharp zigzags. The other tracks plodded along like a snake twisting from side to side and back again. A little to the left. A little to the right. I closely followed the twisting tracks being careful not to let my arms squish their paths.

I spun around. I moved back away from the tracks, so I could see the whole scene. With one arm, I traced the gosling tracks. With another, I traced the path the other tracks made.

Closer.

Closer.

Closer.

SQUELCH.

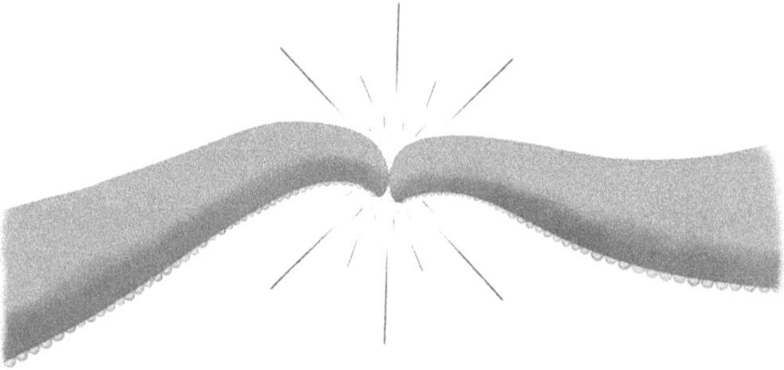

The suckers on the tips of my arms collided. It was just as I suspected.

The two eggs ran into each other!

I continued around the eggshells to make sure. There it was in the damp ground. Proof.

Two butt prints surrounded by eggshell parts.

From there, I saw two sets of tracks side-by-side heading towards the water's edge. Two mysteries solved. But our case wasn't over. Now we had two young ones out alone and it was going to get dark fast.

The sun was inching toward the horizon. I wasn't going to be able to find these young ones on my own in time. I needed help. I needed a search party.

"Tank, Lightning," I called them both over. "I'll follow the tracks, but if they lead to the water, the young ones could be anywhere. Let's organize this crowd into teams to search the lake. Lightning, take a team to search from the sky toward Mama

Goo's. Tank, you take a team and search the lake edge toward the platypus den."

"On it, Octo!" Lightning said. She flitted over to the crowd.

"I'll ask the frogs to check the lily pad garden," Tank said. "And I'll send the turtles to inspect the old beaver den."

"Thanks, team!" I shouted over the crowd. I heard Lightning rounding up a group of birds. She explained that they would fly in a line towards the waterfowl habitat and Mama Goo's. The frogs and the turtles were nodding as Tank outlined the plan. Everyone was getting to work. It was time for me to get back to searching too.

I inspected the area around the eggshells again. Both sets of tracks led straight toward the lake. I followed them right up to the edge, where they disappeared.

The puggle and the gosling had gone into the lake.

9

My spectacles weren't needed in the water. I tucked them away with my notebook and pens. There's no way to describe how wonderful it feels to be surrounded by water. Especially after missing my morning swim.

Even though the water was murky, my eyes adjusted perfectly. Without the tracks, I needed something else to follow. I curled my arms on the lake bottom. Then I looked around for disturbances in the water. Ripples, plants moving, or splashes could be a clue. I was looking for anything.

I waited and watched.

I watched and waited.

Then I waited and watched some more.

Maybe the search party found something, I thought.

I started to rise to the surface when I saw movement out of the corner of my eye. Tiny little bubbles leading farther into the lake.

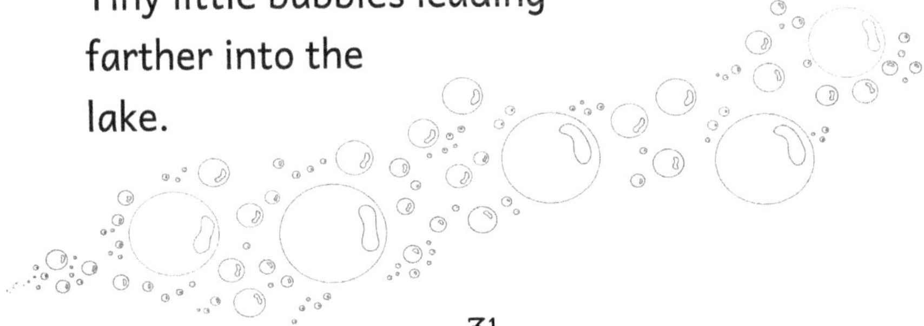

I spun carefully above the muck. I didn't want a big cloud of mud to scare them. I quickly swam off in their direction.

Then I heard someone say, "Don't look now, but something funny-looking is swimming towards us!"

I turned on my jets. Swimming was so much faster than my coconut ride. As I moved closer through the murky water, I saw not one, not two, not three, not four, not five, but six webbed feet! Two gosling and four puggle. I had found them!

"Why is it following us?" one voice said.

"Maybe it wants to eat us!" the other replied.

This new development was putting a kink in closing this case. If they were being chased, I needed to get them home on the double. I had to help them. I sped off at top speed.

"Hurry, it's getting closer!" the first voice said.

As I swam, I searched the water for who was following them. All I could see was their webbed feet. Who was chasing them?

Then it hit me like a wave of water in a hurricane.

It was me. I was chasing them. They didn't know everyone was looking for them. They didn't know that I was here to help. Since they hatched, they'd probably only seen each other. They were two-legged and four-legged creatures. Then here I come, swimming towards them with my eight appendages. No wonder they were rushing away. I probably did look pretty funny to them. Maybe scary, too.

I needed to think. If I sped toward them, I could scare them again and they would swim farther away. If I reached one arm up slowly, the gosling might think it was a worm and that would be quite unpleasant. This **aspect** of the case was proving to be hard to crack.

Side Note:
An aspect is a piece, a part, or a feature of something. For example, part of a missing eggs case.

I needed help. Thankfully, Tank had invented just the thing for this murky situation. I swam up to the surface behind a patch of cattails. From my hat, I pulled out an emergency signal beacon. I pointed the beacon towards the sky and pushed the eject button. A shower of small purple flowers shot up into the air. They took flight on the wind across the lake.

I hope Lightning sees the signal, I thought.

While I waited, I watched the young ones play together.

They swam around each other, splashing and laughing. They were becoming the best of friends.

"Hiya, Octo, I saw your signal! We haven't found the puggle and the gosling yet, but I was hoping that the signal meant that you had. So, have you? Have you found them?"

"Hi, Lightning, thanks for coming. Yes, I found them, but I need a little help getting them back to shore." I pointed to where the young ones were playing. Lightning flew right over to them. When they started following her back to their mothers, I dove back under the surface, taking their path of bubbles to the muddy shoreline.

10

As the gosling and puggle came into view of the lakeshore, everyone heard Mama Goo's honking. Those who didn't would be able to catch it on the news. The camera team was on the scene. They followed the mothers out to their babies.

I didn't want to disturb their reunion. So instead, I swam around and came up on the banks next to Tank. Neither of us like the spotlight.

"That goose has one loud honk," Tank said.

I looked over at my assistant. He kept one eye on the reunion and one eye searching the tall grasses that could cover our exit. The young ones were back with their mothers. Our case was closed. The idea of slipping away for a nice seawater swim to end the day was very tempting. But the job wasn't quite finished.

"Hiya, Octo! Hiya, Tank!" Lightning flew over and hovered next to a cattail. "The gosling and puggle are safe and sound and with their moms. You solved it, Octo! I knew you would. You always do. Best case closer at the ZAR&R, that's for sure!"

"Thanks, Lightning," I said, smiling. "I couldn't have done it without such a great team."

Before any of us could say anything else, I heard Mama Goo honking my name.

"Octo! Octo! Where are you? Octo!"

To save everyone's ears, Lightning flew up and showed her over. The mothers and young ones swam to the shore.

"There you are, Octo! I wanted," Mama Goo paused. She nodded to River. "Well, we wanted to say thank you and introduce our little ones. Thank you for getting them back home safely."

"All in a day's work," I said. "Nice to finally meet you two. You both are already very popular around here."

"You have a lot of arms," the puggle said.

"Eight, to be exact," I replied.

River snuggled her puggle.

"Already so curious," she said. "Thank you, Octo. I'm glad we met today."

"As am I," I replied. "Come by my home office if there is ever anything else you need."

She nodded gently before she and her puggle disappeared underwater.

"Mama Goo," I began to say, but she interrupted me.

"Oh, Octo," she said, sighing. She looked like she had something to say. It seemed she couldn't decide on the words she wanted to use. Mama Goo was speechless for a third time today. That was definitely a record.

We both nodded toward each other. She took her gosling under her wing and they both swam back to their nest.

"Great work today, team," I said to Tank and Lightning. "Let's go home and get some rest."

"Because who knows what mysteries there will be tomorrow, right, Octo? It could be anything! Maybe in the grasslands or in the aquarium? I should get the buzz on that side of the ZAR&R and that way we will be on top of the scoop when it drops."

"Sounds good, Lightning." I waved with one of my arms as she flitted off. "Tank, do you think you could work on something that will help get mud out of suckers?" I asked.

Tank lit up bright blue as he always did when he got an idea.

"I'll get right on it, boss!" he said.

"You'll probably be needing these."

Tank dropped my coconut shells out of a basket on his ride and then turned to head for home.

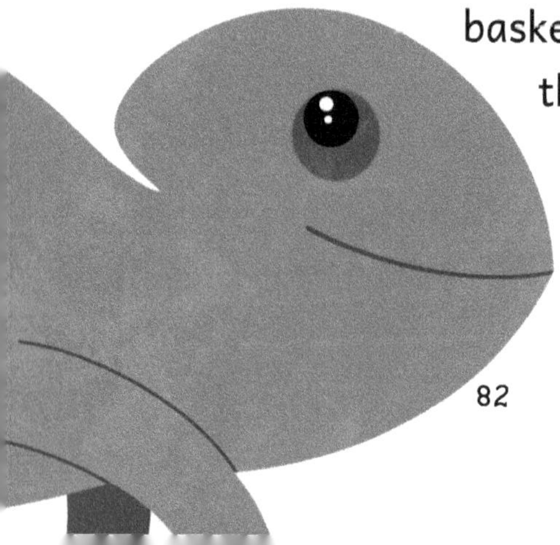

Home. I was ready to get

back to my home office. I pulled myself into my coconut shells and sped away from the lake. That seawater swim was singing to me, and I couldn't wait to finish the song.

NEW RECORDING
1 MINUTE 8 SECONDS

Is this on?

Hello?

Okay, it's on.

Good.

Everything went back to normal around here. All in time for a good night's sleep.

All of the other eggs hatched normally. I'm working on something to help catch any walking eggs. Just as a safety measure for the future. We don't want any more young ones wandering off. Or any more residents being falsely accused of gosling–napping.

Mama Goo was so glad to have her gosling back. She brought baskets filled with our favorites to Octo's place. I ate so many grasshopper cupcakes, the only shade I could turn was green. Mmm, I'm still licking my lips from that feast.

Word around the pond is that she baked dozens and dozens of crawfish cookies too. She dropped them off at the platypus den. After Mama Goo accused River of taking her egg, the cookies must have been her way of saying sorry.

Okay, well, that brings this case to a close. I'm going to grab one last cupcake and blend in somewhere. (Don't worry, not in Octo's clamshell chair. I don't want to be covered in octopus ink.)

What are the Facts?

What are the true animal facts in this book?

Well, I'm glad you asked. Some of the things in the book are very true and some are very made-up. You probably already know that animals don't communicate the way we do. For example, they don't use words or speak our language. They also don't solve cases at zoos and aquariums. ***(That we know of!)***

Here are animal facts from this book that are true:

- Hummingbirds are super fast! They beat their wings at over 3,000 times a minute! They can fly up to 75 miles per hour, but can stop in an instant.

- Chameleons' eyes move in two different directions at once. But when a chameleon sees something it wants to eat with one eye, the other eye will swivel to focus so it can shoot its tongue out and snag lunch.

- There are octopuses that use coconut shells to get around, but they do it all underwater.
  Yes, the plural of octopus is octopuses.

- Red pandas can, and do, walk down trees headfirst. Don't try this at home!

- A platypus is a mammal with a beak, fur, and webbed feet. Platypuses usually lay 1-3 eggs at a time. Puggles hatch after about 10 days.

And here are some that were changed and created for this story:

- Chameleons don't change the color of their skin. They have tiny micro-crystals on top of their skin that they can move closer together and further apart to reflect different wavelengths of light– and that makes them look like they are changing colors. So, sadly, a real chameleon won't blend into your clamshell chair.

- Octopuses can survive on land, but not for very long. Octo, PI, is a special character who can thrive in both environments.

- Octopuses' habitats are in saltwater locations. They are very, very rarely found in fresh bodies of water.

- Speaking of where animals live, platypuses are more likely to be found in rivers and streams than lakes and ponds.

- Platypus eggs are leathery, not hard like chicken or goose eggs. To hatch, puggles use a tiny tooth to break through that they lose as they get bigger. Adult platypuses don't have any teeth!

- Puggles are very, very tiny when they hatch. They are about the size of a little lima bean and they don't leave the den for a few months after they hatch.

- The ZAR&R is not a real place you can visit, but there are many places like it around the world that help animals get what they need so that they can live their life in the wild again.

More

A ZAR&R Mystery

OCTO, PI

Coming soon!

The Residents of the ZAR&R in this Book

Octo, PI

Species: Veined Octopus
Pronouns: she/her

Height: 12 in
Weight: 1 lb
Habitat: Sandy Beach
Special Skills: Solving Mysteries
Favorite Food: Crab Crumpets
Been at the ZAR&R for: 3 years

Tank

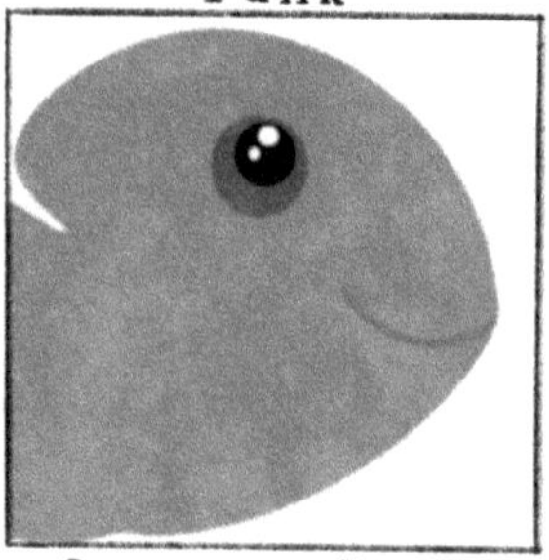

Species: Chameleon
Pronouns: he/him

Height: 21 in
Weight: 14 oz
Habitat: Rain Forest
Special Skills: Inventing Things
Favorite Food: Grasshopper Cupcakes
Been at the ZAR&R for: 8 years

Lightning

Species: Hummingbird
Pronouns: she/her

Height: 3 in
Weight: 2.5 g
Habitat: Woods
Special Skills: Talking Fast
Favorite Food: Honeysuckle Nectar
Been at the ZAR&R for: 1 year

Mama Goo

Species: Canada Goose

Pronouns: she/her

Height: 30 in
Weight: 9 lbs
Habitat: Pond
Special Skills: Baking Pastries
Favorite Food: Berries
Been at the ZAR&R for: 10 years

Puck & Pan

Species: Red Panda

Pronouns: he/him

	Puck	Pan
Height:	24 in	23 in
Weight:	11 lbs	10 lbs

Habitat: Forest
Special Skills: Playing Tricks
Favorite Food: Bamboo
Been at the ZAR&R for: 3 years

River

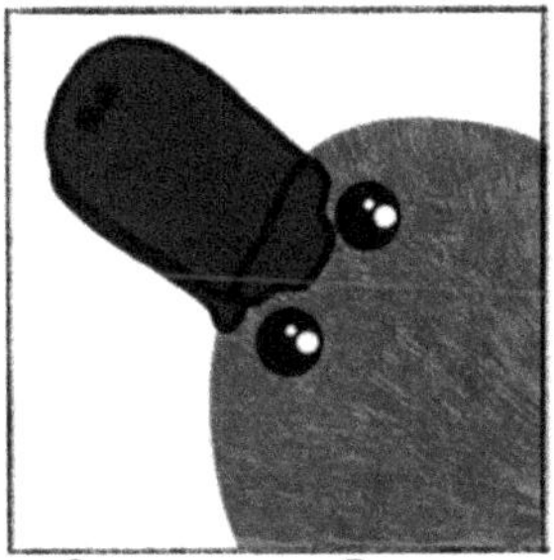

Species: Platypus

Pronouns: she/her

Height: 18 in
Weight: 2.5 lbs
Habitat: Wetlands
Special Skills: First Aid
Favorite Food: Shellfish
Been at the ZAR&R for: 1 week

Steel

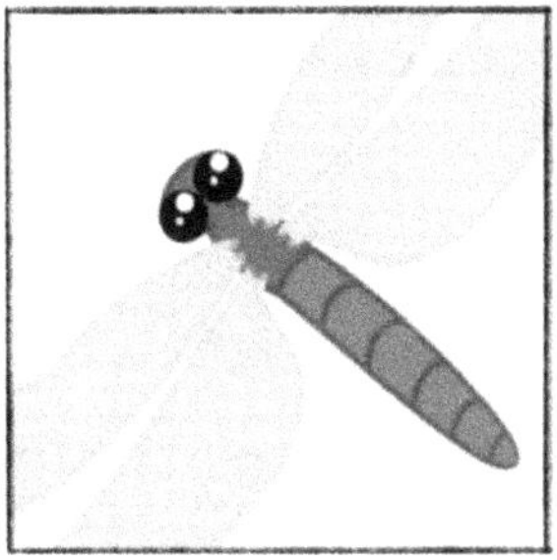

Species: Dragonfly

Pronouns: he/him

Height: 2 in
Weight: 0.5 g
Habitat: Pond Grass
Special Skills: Steering in Flight
Favorite Food: Mosquito Pie
Been at the ZAR&R for: 1 month

Can you find the residents in the book on the map?

- Octo PI
- Tank
- Lightning
- Mama Goo
- Puck and Pan
- River
- Steel

OTHER THINGS TO FIND:

Where they found the egg shells

Where Octo found the little ones

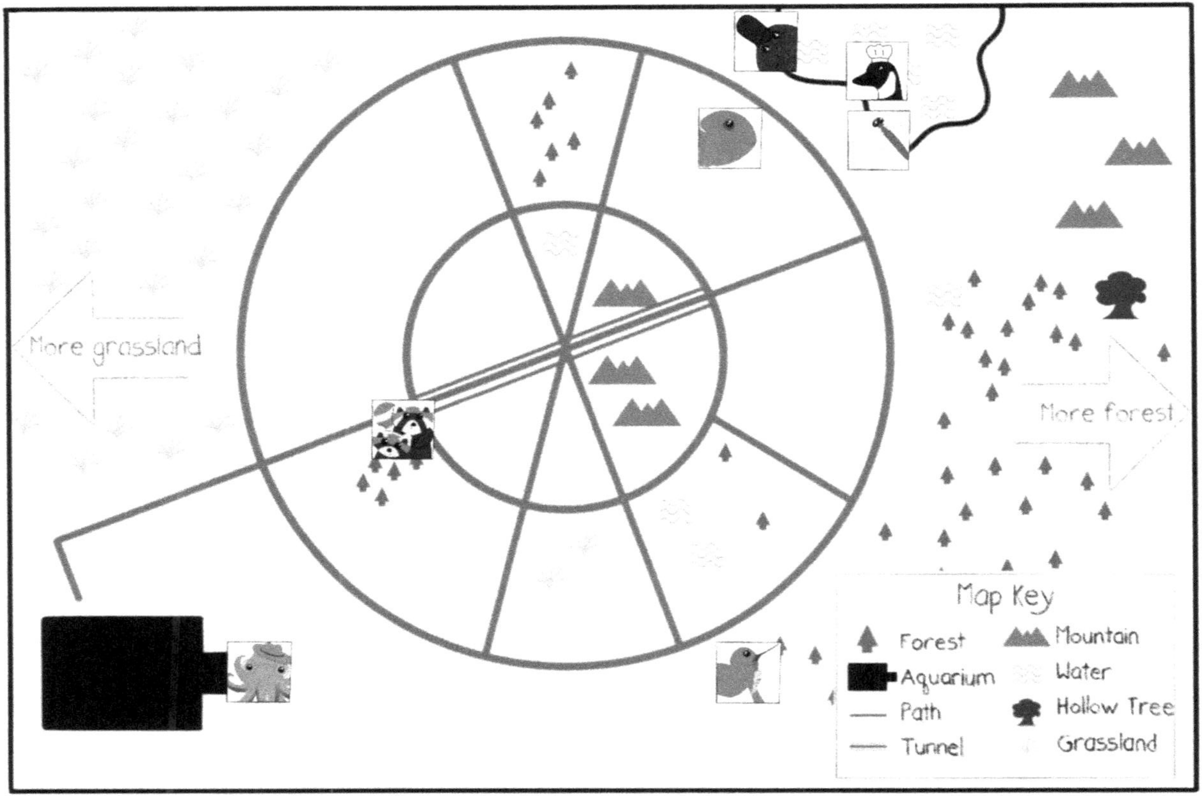
More grassland
More forest
Map Key
Forest
Aquarium
Path
Tunnel
Mountain
Water
Hollow Tree
Grassland

Included Pages:

- About your character
- 3 Fun Things
- A map of the ZAR&R
- A poem by character
- Real animal fact sheet

https://subscribepage.io/minizinetemplate

Help Octo, PI, Out

Even though a lot of people read this book before we published it, you still might find things that are wrong, like grammar mistakes or misspelled words.

If you found a mistake, ask an adult to scan the QR code below, or visit the link, and you can let Octo know what it is and where to find it so she can fix it in the next edition.

https://wondercreekmedia.com/helpocto

ABOUT THE AUTHOR

Sarah McDavis loves bringing stories to life. The first story she told was the thrilling tale of the town of PLOP. Unfortunately, she was three, unable to write it down and can no longer remember the plot. Thankfully, Sarah has learned that superskill and handwrites (or dictates!) all her first drafts.

Since there aren't any humans at the ZAR&R, Sarah can't live there so she lives in Pittsburgh, PA. Luckily though, she can visit the ZAR&R anytime and talk with the residents. If they keep telling her stories, she'll keep telling you.

You can find out more about Sarah at her website:
www.sarahmcdavis.com

Milton Keynes UK
Ingram Content Group UK Ltd.
UKHW022155290524
443431UK00013B/301

9 798990 515802